Great Inventions

THE COMPUTER

by Gayle Worland

Consultant:
George Keremedjiev
Director, American Computer Museum
Bozeman, Montana

Capstone
press

Mankato, Minnesota

Fact Finders is published by Capstone Press
151 Good Counsel Drive, P.O. Box 669, Mankato, Minnesota 56002
http://www.capstone-press.com

Library of Congress Cataloging-in-Publication Data
Worland, Gayle.
    The computer / Gayle Worland.
    p. cm.—(Fact finders. Great inventions)
    Includes bibliographical references (p. 31) and index.
    Contents: Man versus machine—Before the computer—Inventors—The computer
changes—How a computer works—Computers today.
    ISBN 0-7368-2215-1 (hardcover)
    1. Computers—Juvenile literature. [1. Computers.] I. Title. II. Series.
QA76.5 .W668 2004
004—dc21   2002156502

Editorial Credits
Roberta Schmidt, editor; Juliette Peters, series designer and illustrator; Alta Schaffer,
    photo researcher; Eric Kudalis, product planning editor

Photo Credits
Bruce Coleman Inc., 16
Corbis/Bettmann, 6–7, 12, 13, 18; Charles E. Rotkin, 14–15; James A. Sugar, 17;
    Roger Ressmeyer, 19; Saba/Najlah Feanny, 4–5
Hulton/Archive Photos by Getty Images, 9, 10
IBM Corporate Archives, 27 (left)
PhotoDisc Inc., 1, 21, 24, 27 (right); Jules Frazier, cover
Smithsonian Institution, neg. #90-5951, 26 (middle); neg. #88-19284, 26 (right);
    neg. #91-14187, 27 (middle)
Stock Montage Inc., 11
U.S. Army Photo, 26 (left)

1 2 3 4 5 6 08 07 06 05 04 03

Table of Contents

Chapter 1

Man versus Machine

In 1997, people around the world watched an unusual chess game. World Chess Champion Garry Kasparov was playing against a computer.

Kasparov had played chess with a computer before. In 1996, he beat the computer. This time, the engineers at International Business Machines (IBM) were sure their computer would win.

The computer was named Deep Blue. It could look at 200 million possible chess moves per second.

Deep Blue and Kasparov played several games. Deep Blue won the match.

Garry Kasparov played chess against an IBM computer named Deep Blue. The man on the right moved the chess pieces where Deep Blue chose to go.

Many people wondered if the chess match was a sign of the future. Would computers someday be smarter than people? Other people said to remember that people make computers. The machines are tools to make life easier.

Chapter 2

Before the Computer

People have always looked for ways to make work easier. Before the computer, people built tools and machines to help them solve math problems.

The Abacus

The wooden abacus was the first tool that helped people solve math problems. It was invented in ancient Asia. The abacus has a rectangular wooden frame. Rods with beads cross the wooden frame. People used the abacus to add and subtract by moving beads up and down the rods.

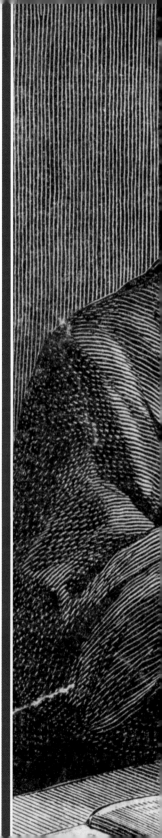

People used the abacus to add and subtract numbers.

7

Chapter 3

Inventors

The computer was not invented by one person. Many people and many years of tests and discoveries helped make the modern computer.

Blaise Pascal

In 1642, Blaise Pascal invented a mechanical calculator. His calculator used gears and levers to add and subtract numbers.

Pascal's invention worked much like an odometer. An odometer adds up the miles or kilometers that a car has been driven.

Blaise Pascal was a French mathematician.

Charles Babbage was a British inventor.

Charles Babbage

In 1832, Charles Babbage designed a new machine. He called it the Analytical Engine. He designed it to solve more than one math problem. He wanted his machine to calculate many problems and remember them.

Babbage tried hard to build his machine. But he could not get all of the machine's parts to fit together. The gears and wheels got stuck and would not work.

Babbage never finished the Analytical Engine. But more than 100 years later, other inventors used his ideas.

Babbage's Analytical Engine was powered by steam.

George R. Stibitz

In 1937, American mathematician George R. Stibitz invented the first electric binary adder. This machine used only 1s and 0s to solve math problems. Stibitz's idea was used in later computers. The 1s and 0s then were called bits.

Howard H. Aiken

In 1944, Howard H. Aiken built the first electric calculator. This calculator was nicknamed the Mark I. The Mark I was as long as half of a football field. It used 500 miles (805 kilometers) of wires.

Eckert and Mauchly

In 1942, John Presper Eckert and John W. Mauchly started to build a new machine. Four years later, they finished the first programmable general purpose electronic computer. It was as big as two small houses and weighed 30 tons (27 metric tons). They called it the ENIAC. ENIAC stands for Electronic Numerical Integrator and Computer.

Aiken used punched paper tapes to make the Mark I (behind him) work.

The ENIAC used a lot of electricity. The lights in the nearby town dimmed whenever the computer was being used.

The ENIAC was an important step in computer history. It could calculate numbers 1,000 times faster than a person using an abacus. It could solve 5,000 additions and 360 to 500 multiplications each minute.

Many people helped Eckert and Mauchly run the ENIAC.

Chapter 4

The Computer Changes

After the mid-1900s, people began to build better computers. They made smaller computers that worked faster than the ENIAC. These computers also could do more than solve math problems.

The Transistor and Microchip

Early computers used glass containers called vacuum tubes. These tubes controlled the electric signals. But vacuum tubes needed a lot of electricity. They also got very hot and broke easily. Computers needed a better way to control the signals.

Most of the early computers were used only by the military. Later, computers became more popular. Many businesses started to use computers.

DATA PROCESSING SYSTEM

In the mid-1900s, hospitals started to use computers to store important information.

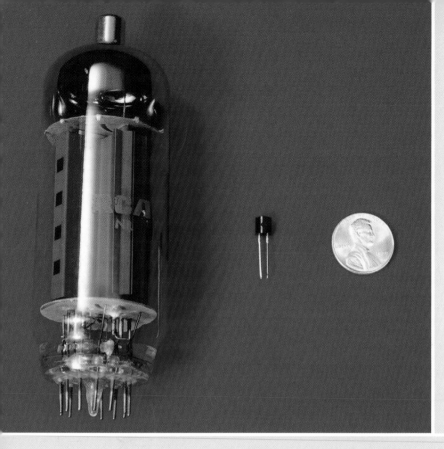

A transistor (middle) is much smaller than a vacuum tube (left). It is also smaller than a penny.

The invention of the transistor in 1947 changed computers forever. A transistor was much smaller, cheaper, and stronger than a vacuum tube. Because of the transistor, computers could be made much smaller and lighter.

After the transistor, computers changed even more. In the late 1950s, scientists found a way to make a computer "chip."

The first computers to use microprocessors appeared in the early 1970s. Many of these computers came as kits. One of these early kit computers was the Altair 8800.

This chip could store a lot of information in a very small space. By 1971, scientists were able to put most of the computer's calculating parts on a chip smaller than a fingernail. Thousands of transistors now could fit onto this "microchip" called the microprocessor.

As the transistor and the microchip got smaller, so did computers. A computer could sit on a desk instead of filling a large room.

Microchips are smaller than a fingernail.

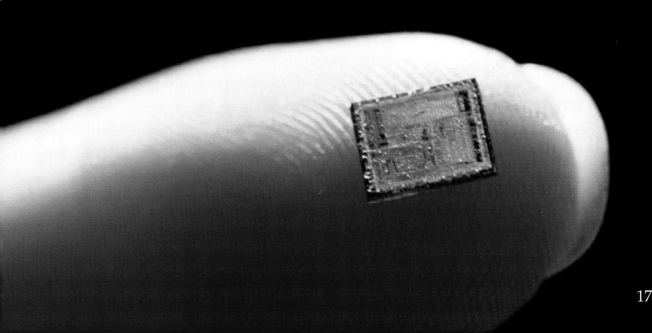

Apple Computers founders Steve Jobs (left) and Stephen Wozniak (right) pose with the company's president John Scully (middle) in 1984.

Personal Computers

In the late 1970s, two men from California changed the computer business. Steve Jobs and Stephen Wozniak decided to make computers that anyone could buy and use. They started Apple Computers. Computers were no longer only for businesses. People could buy computers for their homes.

In 1982, the personal computer was named *Time* magazine's "Man of the Year."

In 1984, Apple Computers made the Macintosh (Mac) computer. This computer had a control called a mouse. The mouse made opening programs easy. The Mac also used icons, or pictures, on the screen. These icons let people use the computer without typing in codes.

Many other companies started to build desktop computers. Computers continued to get smaller and cost less.

In the 1980s, many people bought computers to use at home.

Chapter 5

How a Computer Works

Numbers make computers work. But computers understand only two numbers. These numbers are 0 and 1. They are called binary digits. The different combinations of 0 and 1 tell the computer what to do. A 0 turns off an electric signal. A 1 turns on the electric signal. This on-off switching of electric signals controls everything a computer does. Every letter, number, and picture on the computer has its own set of 0s and 1s.

Decimal number	Binary number
0	0
1	1
2	10
3	11
4	100
5	101
6	110
7	111
8	1000
9	1001
10	1010

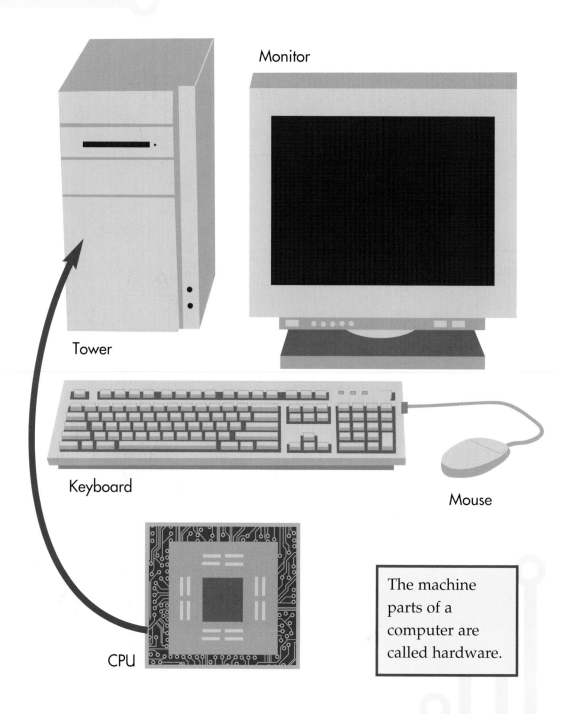

Monitor

Tower

Keyboard

Mouse

CPU

The machine parts of a computer are called hardware.

The Parts of a Computer

Computers are made up of hardware and software. The hardware is the machine. The software is the programs a computer uses.

Today, personal computer hardware includes a monitor, a tower, a keyboard, and a mouse. The monitor is like a TV screen. It shows words and pictures. The tower is the main part of the computer. All of the calculations happen in the tower. The keyboard and mouse let a person tell the computer what to do.

The "heart" or "brain" of a personal computer is the central processing unit (CPU). The CPU is also called a microprocessor. It is located in the tower. The CPU does most of the work. It calculates numbers faster than any person can.

Chapter 6

Computers Today

Today, computers are used almost everywhere. Most people use some kind of computer at their jobs. Checkout clerks at grocery stores use them to scan items and total prices. Police detectives use computers to find information and check fingerprints. Car mechanics test cars with computers. The computer shows what is wrong with a car.

Millions of people use computers for learning. Many libraries and schools have computers. The computers help adults and children find information.

Computers often are used to teach or help find information.

Computers also are used for fun activities. They are used to make and play video games and movies. Computers are also used to make TV shows, cartoons, and commercials.

Some people use computers to commit crimes. Computer "viruses" can make other computers stop working.

Disney's 1995 film *Toy Story* was the first full-length movie made totally by computers. It took about 800,000 computer hours to make the movie.

Computers through the Years

ENIAC
1946

DEC PDP-8
1965

MITS Altair
1975

Some people use computers to steal computer games, programs, or private information.

Computers affect people's lives in many ways. Computers can make work easier. They help people find information and solve problems. Computers are an important tool for the modern world.

IBM PC

1981

Apple Macintosh

1984

a laptop

today

Fast Facts

- Before the computer, many people used an abacus to calculate numbers.

- Charles Babbage designed the Analytical Engine in 1832. His ideas helped the invention of computers more than 100 years later.

- The ENIAC was the first programmable general purpose electronic computer.

- The binary digits 0 and 1 tell a computer what to do. The 0s and 1s are called bits. Eight bits side by side are called a byte.

- The transistor and the microchip helped computers be built smaller and lighter.

- Steve Jobs and Stephen Wozniak started to build and sell personal computers in the late 1970s.

- On September 9, 1945, a moth flew into a computer. The computer stopped working. This moth was the first computer "bug."

Hands On:

Write in Binary

Computers use binary code. You can use binary code to write messages, too.

A	01000001		N	01001110
B	01000010		O	01001111
C	01000011		P	01010000
D	01000100		Q	01010001
E	01000101		R	01010010
F	01000110		S	01010011
G	01000111		T	01010100
H	01001000		U	01010101
I	01001001		V	01010110
J	01001010		W	01010111
K	01001011		X	01011000
L	01001100		Y	01011001
M	01001101		Z	01011010

What you need

pencil   paper   a friend

What you do

1. Write your name in capital letters.
2. Look at the table above. Look at the binary code that stands for each letter in your name.
3. Use the table to write your name in binary code.
4. Write your friend's name in binary code.
5. Send messages to your friend in binary code.

Glossary

abacus (AB-uh-kuhss)—an ancient machine used to add and subtract

calculate (KAL-kyuh-late)—to find a solution by using math

design (di-ZINE)—to draw something that could be built or made

engineer (en-juh-NIHR)—a person who is trained to design and build machines

hardware (HARD-wair)—the "machine" part of a computer

match (MACH)—a game or series of games

microchip (MYE-kroh-chip)—a tiny circuit that processes information in a computer

software (SAWFT-wair)—the programs that tell the hardware of the computer what to do

transistor (tran-ZISS-tur)—a tiny electronic device that controls the flow of electrical current; transistors replaced vacuum tubes in computers.

Internet Sites

Do you want to find out more about the computer?
Let FactHound, our fact-finding hound dog, do the research for you.

Here's how:
1) Visit *http://www.facthound.com*
2) Type in the **Book ID** number:
   0736822151
3) Click on **FETCH IT**.

FactHound will fetch Internet sites picked by our editors just for you!

Read More

Dunn, John M. *The Computer Revolution.* World History. San Diego: Lucent Books, 2002.

Graham, Ian. *Computers.* Technoworld. Austin, Texas: Raintree Steck-Vaughn, 2001.

Sherman, Josepha. *The History of the Personal Computer.* Watts Library. New York: Franklin Watts, 2003.

Williams, Brian. *Computers.* Great Inventions. Chicago: Heinemann, 2002.

Index